God's Amazing Book

by Kathleen Ruckman   Illustrated by Lauretta Davies

This book is dedicated to our dear friend, Nina Murff, who loved children, and who loved the Word of God. Nina is now with the Lord, but thoughts of her are held in our hearts and we miss her.
—Kathleen and Lauretta

Editor: Karen Rhodes
Creative Director: Curtis D. Corzine
Art Direction & Layout: Kevin Spear
Printed in Singapore

Warner
Press Kids
educate • nurture • inspire

God gave us an amazing Book.
Come with me and take a look!
God's Word is written for us to see,
The Bible is special to you and me!

God wrote a Love Letter long ago
To tell me that He loves me so!
The words in the Bible help me to see
What a wonderful Love Letter God wrote to me!

God loved the world so
much that he gave his one
and only Son. Anyone
who believes in him will
not die but will have
eternal life.   John 3:16 (NIrV)

When I walk in the dark, I can't see where to go.
I get off the path, even stubbing my toe!
But just like a flashlight that helps me to see,
God's Word lights the path for you and for me!

Your word is like a lamp that shows
me the way. It is like a light that
guides me.   Psalm 119:105 (NIrV)

In springtime my mother plants seeds in the ground.
She pushes them deep and they cannot be found.
God's words are like seeds planted deep in my heart.
They help me to grow—right from the start!

*Grow in the grace and knowledge of
our Lord and Savior Jesus Christ.*
2 Peter 3:18 (NIV)

When I take a bath, soap cleans me all up.
It even cleans up my new little pup!
God's Word is like soap—it washes me too
By teaching me just what Jesus would do.

How can a young person keep his life pure? By living in keeping with your word.

Psalm 119:9 (NIrV)

When I walk in the woods, there are pathways to take.
I pray, "Jesus, help me to make no mistake."
The Bible's my road map. It helps me to see
Where God, who knows *best*, always leads me.

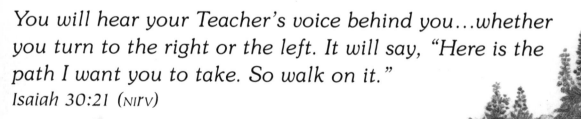

You will hear your Teacher's voice behind you...whether
you turn to the right or the left. It will say, "Here is the
path I want you to take. So walk on it."
Isaiah 30:21 (NIrV)

If *millions* of piggy banks were emptied, I'm told—
Coins stacked to the sky in bright, shiny gold—
They couldn't compare to the riches I find
When I let God's words fill my heart and my mind!

They are more precious than gold, than much pure gold.   Psalm 19:10 (NIV)

Did you ever eat jam on your bread, nice and sweet?
Or how about honey, that sweet, sticky treat?
God's words in the Bible are sweeter than honey.
I keep wanting more to fill up my tummy!

Your words are very sweet to my taste! They are sweeter than honey to me. *Psalm 119:103 (NIrV)*

God's Word, like a mirror, helps me to see,
The deeper, *forever*, part of me!
When I read the Bible, it helps me to find,
How I should live and what God has in mind.

Take a good look at the perfect law [God's mirror]…
Keep looking at it…do what the law says. Then you will
be blessed in what you do. James 1:25 (NIrV)

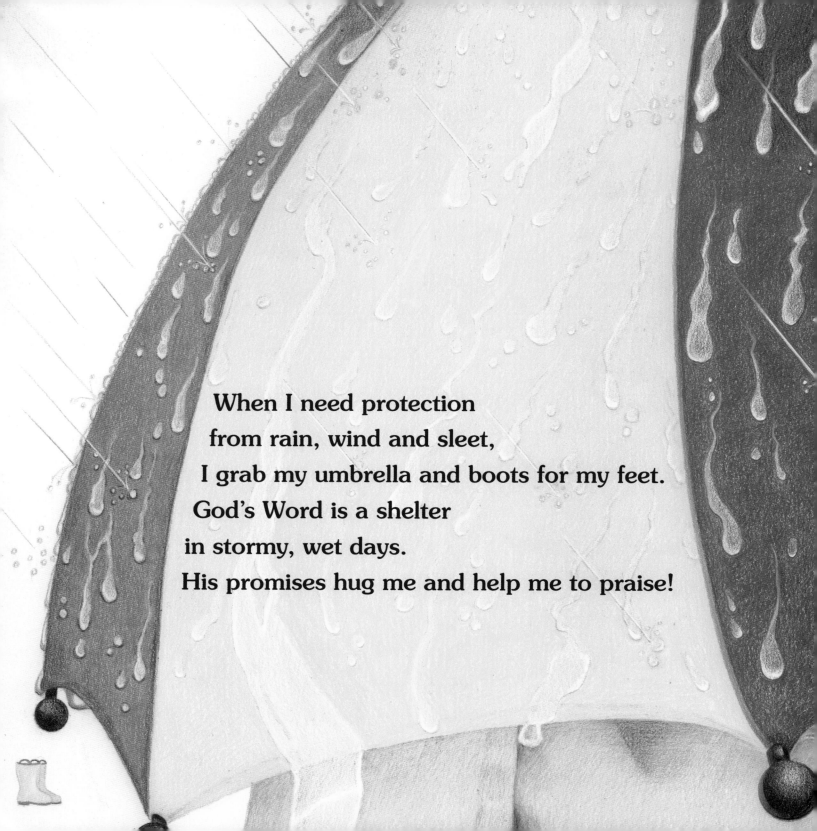

When I need protection
from rain, wind and sleet,
I grab my umbrella and boots for my feet.
God's Word is a shelter
in stormy, wet days.
His promises hug me and help me to praise!

You have been a place to hide
when storms came.
Isaiah 25:4 (NIrV)

God's words are like notes in a *whi-stl-ing* song.
They sing in my heart—all the day long!
When I'm scared or sad every once in awhile,
God's words are like music! They make me smile!

No matter where I live, I sing.   Psalm 119:54 (NIrV)

God wanted to show me His love here on earth,
So He came to us all in a sweet Baby's birth!
His name is Jesus, and He is God's Son,
Born in a manger—the Wonderful One!

Jesus died on a cross for me and for you.
He came back to life; I know this is true!
He takes my hand to show me the way.
Jesus, the Word, in my heart here to stay!

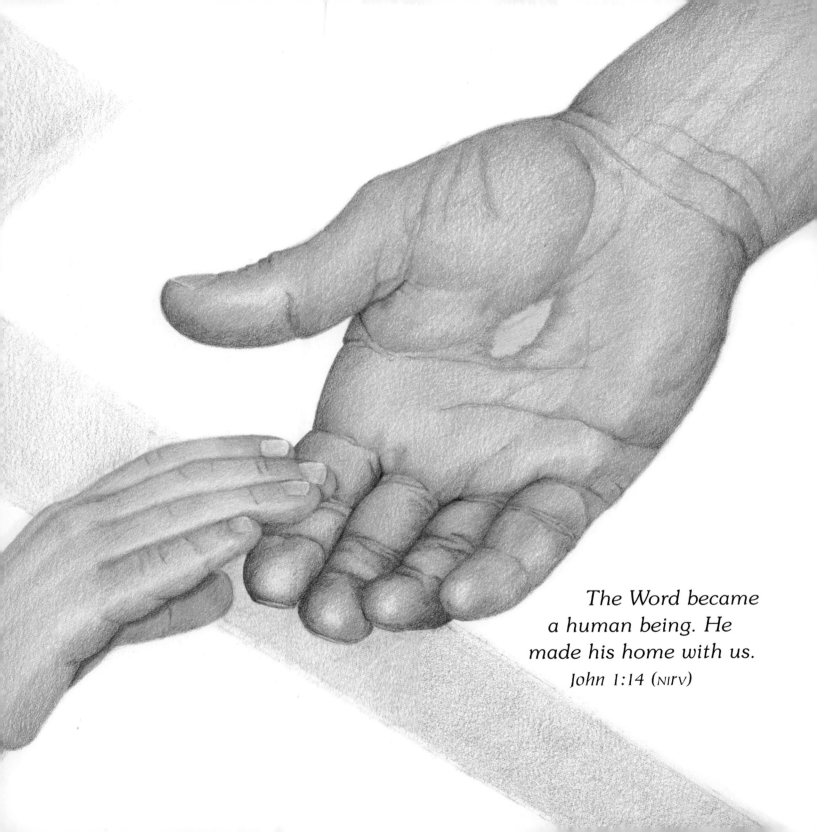

The Word became
a human being. He
made his home with us.

John 1:14 (NIrV)

The Bible is a gift from heaven above.

God gave me this gift with a heart full of love.

What better gift can I give to a friend?

God's Word is forever! Its truth has no end!

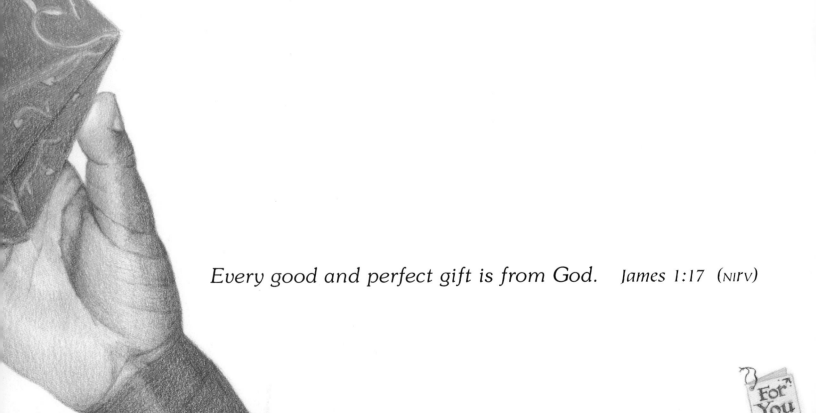

Every good and perfect gift is from God.   James 1:17 (NIrV)

Note To Parents And Teachers

Open your Bible and show children the passages to help them become familiar with the Bible.
Read the scriptures out loud together, as you remind your children, "God's Word is like…"
Personalize the descriptions with the pronoun, "you."

 The Bible is like a love letter to you: Read John 3:16

 God's Word guides your steps like a flashlight in the dark: Read Psalm 119:105

 The words in the Bible are like seeds; they help you to grow: Read 2 Peter 3:18

 God's Word helps keep your heart clean when you read and obey it: Read Psalm 119:9

 The Bible is like a map when you don't know which way to turn: Read Isaiah 30:21

 The words in the Bible are more precious to you than gold: Read Psalm 19:10

 The words in the Bible are much sweeter to you than honey: Read Psalm 119:103

 The Bible is like a mirror; it helps you see how to live like Jesus: Read James 1:25

 God's Word protects you, like an umbrella in a storm: Read Isaiah 25:4

 The words in the Bible are like notes in a song and music in your heart: Read Psalm 119:54

 Jesus is God who came to earth because He loves you! Jesus is the Living Word.   Read John 1:14

 The Bible is a gift from God so you can read it, keep its words in your heart and become friends with God.   Read James 1:17